STUDY GUIDE

The Intimate Marriage

R.C. Sproul

I0806868

LIGONIER MINISTRIES

Renew your Mind.

LIGONIER.ORG | 800-435-4343

421 Ligonier Court, Sanford, FL 32771
E-mail: info@ligonier.org

Printed in China.

1

What Is Marriage?

OUTLINE

I. Marriage is ordained and instituted by God.
   A. Marriage was not created by men.
   B. The origin of marriage:
      i. At every stage of creation, God pronounced a benediction.
      ii. The only malediction was spoken when God saw man was alone (Gen. 2:18).

II. Marriage provides an answer to human loneliness.
   A. Loneliness is one of man's worst pains.
   B. Man and woman are created as sexual creatures designed to complement each other in a relationship of intimacy.
   C. God created women as a special act of creation, not as an after thought or an inferior, but as an equal partner.
   D. God ordained that a man should *cleave* to his wife.
      i. *Cleaving* has nothing to do with a sense of bondage.
      ii. Human fulfillment and intimacy is the reason for cleaving.

III. Marriage is regulated by God's commandments.
   A. God does not abandon His sovereign authority over marriage.
   B. Marriage is a *covenant*.
      i. A covenant is an agreement between two or more parties which has at its heart a promise and contains provisions and stipulations undertaken in the presence of witnesses.
      ii. The covenantal idea is seen in the formal vows in the wedding.
   C. Marriage is the most dangerous institution we have.
      i. Our highest emotional expectations are totally vulnerable in our marriages.
      ii. The possibility of great happiness or terrible hurt exists.

iii. Everything depends on our commitment.
iv. We have lost the sacred and holy character of the vow.

DISCUSSION QUESTIONS

1. Do most people have an honest picture of marriage before they get married? What are some common misconceptions about marriage today?

2. How important is romance to a marriage? What special things keep the romance alive in your marriage?

3. What is the most important vow you have made (will want to make) to your spouse? Have you kept it faithfully? Why is this one so important to you? What can you do this week to further demonstrate your desire to fulfill this sacred trust?

4. How should knowing that our marriages are controlled by God make a difference in the way we:
   a. treat our spouses?
   b. view our marriage commitment?
   c. open our inner selves to our spouses?
   d. view our responsibilities as marriage partners?

5. What do you think are the main reasons why the institution of marriage is in trouble today?

6. What elements in society have a destructive influence on marriage today?

7. What are your reactions when you hear that marriage is the most dangerous institution we have? Explain some of the dangers in marriage.

8. Why do people fear marriage? Why do people not want to get married, although they are willing to live with one another?

9. Do you feel divorce is too easy to obtain in today's society? Why are there more divorces today than ever before? What would have kept "bad" marriages together several generations ago?

2

God and Nakedness

OUTLINE

I. Nakedness carries significance in the Bible.
  A. Nakedness was recast during the creation account (Gen. 2:23-25).
    i. In the first state man was naked and not ashamed (v.25).
    ii. After the fall Adam and Eve hid because they were naked.
      a. The first experience of human guilt was because they were naked.
      b. The confession of their nakedness was a confession of their awareness of sin.
      c. There is a connection between nakedness and guilt.
  B. Noah's nakedness caused his son to dishonor him (Gen. 9:20-27).
  C. Victorious armies used to parade their prisoners nude to increase their humiliation.

II. Nakedness pervades society today.
  A. Nudity is popular: pornography, sexual freedom, etc.
  B. We have ambivalent feelings toward nakedness.
  C. We look for a place where we can be naked, yet without shame.

III. The covering of our nakedness was perfected by God.
  A. The first act of redemption was when God clothed His fallen creatures.
    i. The Atonement centers on covering.
    ii. Christ is the covering for our sins.
  B. God allows us to wear clothes.
    i. There is a connection between physical and emotional nakedness.
    ii. We don't have to reveal our innermost being to everyone.

IV. There are two places where we can be naked and unashamed:
  A. In God's presence.
    i. We can't fool God; therefore, we might as well be totally honest.
    ii. The God who knows me in all of my nakedness loves me.

B. In the holy bond of marriage.
   i. We can be ourselves with our families in an atmosphere of love.
   ii. It is significant to have the person who knows us the best love us the most.
   iii. Marriage is the supreme image that God uses to communicate to His people the relationship He wants with them.
      a. The church is the bride of Christ.
      b. It demonstrates intimacy and deep communion.
   iv. The liberties and benefits of marriage.
      a. God has given us an institution with safeguards and responsibilities and says, "Here you can be naked."
         Don't prevent your partner from knowing you.
         Learn to know each other.
      b. In divorce the person who knows you best rejects you.

DISCUSSION QUESTIONS

1. How do various media influence our concept of morality and acceptable sexual behavior? What should Christians do about this strong influence?

2. How do you feel knowing that you can be totally honest before God because He knows your every thought and feeling? How can such knowledge encourage you in your marriage?

3. What emotions would people experience if they knew they could be totally open and unashamed of their nakedness in their marriages?

4. What three things can we do to promote a more open relationship in our marriages?

5. In what ways has the sexual revolution helped society and the church? How has it been a destructive force to both?

6. Why do you think God clothed Adam and Eve after the Fall? Why couldn't He have merely provided a means of spiritual redemption, leaving physical nakedness out of the picture? What does such an act say about the sanctity of our bodies?

7. Why do you think God uses marriage as the supreme way to communicate the relationship He wants to have with His people? What features are in a marriage that make this the ideal analogy?

8. What is necessary in a relationship before one is comfortable in letting down all defenses? Is complete openness ever possible in a marriage?

3

Knowing One Another

OUTLINE

I. It's important to fully comprehend what God means by *knowing*.
   A. The use of the verb "to know" is significant in the Old Testament.
      i. *Knowing* speaks of the deepest level of human intimacy.
      ii. For intimacy to be possible, knowledge has to take place.
   B. If we are to experience intimacy in our marriages, we have to get to know our partners.
      i. Marriage cannot be continued and sustained by feelings alone.
      ii. Knowing anything requires study.
         a. The two biggest priorities in a man's life are his marriage and his career.
         b. Most men spend little time or energy preparing for marriage or getting to know their wives.
      iii. Happy marriages don't come from doing what comes naturally.
         a. We can learn a lot by studying a person outwardly.
         b. Real learning must occur at a deeper level.

II. There is a way to "knowing."
   A. If you want to know each other, you have to talk!
      i. You must discuss feelings and ideas, not just commonplace reactions (second level of communication).
      ii. Games can reveal felt needs.
         a. What would I be if I could be something different?
         b. In the mail-order partner game, you can pick the options you would choose in an ideal partner.
   B. Felt needs are not insignificant and must not be neglected.
      i. We are not called to selfless love, but we are not to have selfish love either.
      ii. What are your partner's priority needs?

iii. Try to meet all the top felt needs of your spouse.
iv. If one of your top five felt needs is not being met, it becomes your point of vulnerability.
v. We take for granted the things that are going fine in our marriage and overemphasize our unfulfilled longings.
vi. Communication is vital in determining your partner's felt needs.

DISCUSSION QUESTIONS

1. What is a felt need? How does it differ from a real need? Which is more important? Could one have a felt need that did not correspond to the way things really were? If so, how could a felt need be changed?

2. How important is one's family background to a marriage? How does it affect one's concept of what a marriage is?

3. What three things could you do this week to show your spouse that you sincerely want to get to know him/her better?

4. What ingredients are necessary for a lasting marriage?

5. What would society say are the five most important needs in life? What would today's culture list as the five most important characteristics of a marriage? How would a biblical perspective on these two subjects differ from the world's? How has society infiltrated what we as Christians believe to be the important needs of our lives and our marriages? What can the church do to regain a pure biblical perspective?

6. What are some things that block effective communication? What tendencies characterize a bad conversationalist? What can be done to overcome these characteristics? What can you do to encourage better communication between you and your spouse?

7. Think of the areas of your life that you find difficult to discuss with your spouse? Why do you think you feel this barrier? What do you feel would be necessary before you could be more open about these areas? What steps can you take right now to begin this process?

8. List four things you could do to improve the quality of your communication with your spouse. Also identify any areas that may hinder effective communication between you. What can you do about these? Develop a plan to meet with your spouse on a regular basis just to talk. Make it your goal to get to know each other better.

4

Sexual Problems in Marriage

OUTLINE

I. Issues related to sex are the main reasons given for the breakdown of marriages in the U.S. today.
   A. We make a major transition moving from the premarital context where sex is forbidden to a marital context where sex is commanded by God.
      i. Augustine and others believed that the only moral justification for sex within a marriage is procreation.
      ii. God created people with both body and soul so they might enjoy the proper use of both.
   B. God does not grant absolute sexual freedom even in marriage.
      i. Sexual sin is a serious affront to God's holiness.
      ii. God forbids adultery and fornication.
      iii. God is not against pleasure or human fulfillment, but He understands the sanctity of the intimacy that takes place in marriage.
         a. Sex is not wrong in the proper context.
         b. God created sex; He ordains and regulates it.
         c. It is to be used for a couple's enjoyment.

II. There are indisputably major sexual problems.
   A. One problem is paralysis.
      i. In the male, impotency; in the female, frigidity.
      ii. Fear is the primary cause of these paralyses.
         a. The fear of performance is not helped by "Hollywood" myths.
         b. Other fears legitimately interfere:
            1) the fear of physical abuse,
            2) the fear of discovery, and
            3) the fear of pregnancy.
      iii. Solutions for fear begin with an understanding of God's purpose for sex.

a. Our sexual relationship is not for public display.
b. It must be founded on love.
c. Sex must be an expression of love.
  1) The more we demonstrate love to our partner, the less fear we experience.
  2) Perfect love casts out fear (1 John 4:8).

B. Another problem is guilt.
  i. Husbands often think their wives responded more sexually prior to the wedding than after it.
  ii. While many possibilities exist as to why, one that must be considered is unresolved guilt from participation in premarital sex.
  iii. The only solution to this is the confession of sin.
  iv. God's forgiveness removes guilt.

DISCUSSION QUESTIONS

1. How has the Hollywood image of sex affected our understanding of it? How does this clash with what the Bible says about sex?

2. What can you do to instill a healthy perception of sex in your children? How can you help prevent the sexual problems mentioned in this lecture from happening to your child? How could you prevent your teenager from becoming involved in premarital sex?

3. What might a couple do to overcome a particular fear one of them has developed in their sexual relationship?

4. Why is it so difficult to discuss sexual problems with someone else? What could be done to make it less threatening?

5. What can the church do to prevent the breakup of marriages?

6. What is the difference between guilt and guilt feelings? Which one causes a problem of marriage? How? Which one does the Bible say it would remove and replace with peace?

7. How did the fall in Genesis 3 affect the relationship between the sexes? How did it affect sex?

8. What are some of the major causes of separation and divorce?

9. Read 1 John 1:9-2:2. What does this passage say about our sin and our forgiveness? What encouragement does this provide for us?

5

Criticism and Compliments

OUTLINE

I. There are numerous forces against the home.
   A. The major problems destroying the home according to modern research include the following:
      i. sexual problems,
      ii. money problems, and
      iii. in-law problems.
   B. The most destructive force facing the home today is the human tongue.
      i. The negative things we say to each other do more to contribute to the break-down of trust, love and respect than anything else.
      ii. It may manifest itself in other areas, but the root problem is often the tongue.

II. Do you use the tongue for compliment or criticism?
   A. Song of Solomon 4:1-7 is not an analogy of Christ's love for the church.
      i. This is a divinely inspired love song.
      ii. This is a beautiful compliment of a person honoring his partner.
   B. James 3:5-10 warns against the ravages of the tongue.
      i. The tongue is the most destructive member of the body.
      ii. A thoughtless word can be devastating.
   C. There are exercises to encourage proper use of the tongue.
      i. Write the five most meaningful compliments you have ever received.
      ii. Write the five most painful criticisms you have ever received. (This will show the center of your emotional pain.)

III. What we say to each other in marriage creates the environment of trust, intimacy, and love.
   A. We need to cherish each other.

   i. What we say and do shows how much we cherish each other.
   ii. Nothing can destroy a sense of love faster than an unkind, cutting remark.
   iii. We are called to build one another up.
   iv. Remember—you cannot recall your words.

B. We need to compliment one another.
   i. Be believable and authentic.
   ii. Take time to find something of value in your mate and compliment him/her on that.
   iii. It takes nine authentic compliments to outweigh the pain of one criticism.

DISCUSSION QUESTIONS

1. Read Proverbs 18:20-21. What does this say about the power of the tongue? How does this make you feel?

2. What are some ways people misuse their speech? What can you do to keep your tongue in check?

3. How should Christians respond to severe criticism?

4. What are some compliments you could give your partner in the following areas:
   a. his/her physical life?
   b. his/her emotional life?
   c. his/her spiritual life?

5. What ingredients comprise an encouraging statement? How does a truly encouraging statement affect the recipient?

6. Which has more lasting impact—a word or an act? Why?

7. Why is it so hard to give a compliment? What prohibits us from making them more a part of our speech?

8. In what ways has God encouraged you? How does that make you feel? What is a proper response to these acts of God?

6

Role of Man and Woman

OUTLINE

I. The wife's role is found in Ephesians 5:21-24.

- A. Does Ephesians 5:21 imply a mutual submission?
    - i. The mutual submission interpretation evolved because of today's confusion over the role of women.
    - ii. Every Christian at some point is called to submission.
    - iii. We are to submit in the fear of God.
- B. What does "submit as to the Lord" mean?
    - i. Wives are to submit themselves to their husbands in a manner analogous to how they are to submit themselves to Christ.
    - ii. The husband is the head of the wife in a manner similar to Christ's headship over the church.
        - a. Headship = pre-eminence, leadership, final authority.
        - b. This does not license the husband to be a tyrant or to treat his wife as a slave.
- C. Should a woman always submit herself to her husband?
    - i. This is not an absolute chain of command.
    - ii. God requires that we disobey any authority when obedience means going against God's revealed will.
- D. Does this imply that woman are inferior to men?
    - i. Subordination never implies inferiority.
    - ii. In the work of the Trinity, the Son is subordinate to the Father, and the Spirit is subordinate to the Father and to the Son.
    - iii. The woman was created to be a helpmate, while the man is given the fundamental responsibility for the family.

II. The husband's role is found in Ephesians 5:25: Husbands love your wives as Christ loved the church.

A. Disregard what the Bible says to your partner and concentrate on what it says to you.
B. As the husband fulfills his responsibility, the wife will respond positively to his leadership.
C. God calls the husband to be "Christ" to his wife.
    i. He is to protect her integrity.
    ii. He is to present her whole to Christ.
    iii. He is to nourish her and cherish her.

DISCUSSION QUESTIONS

1. How is the Christian marriage a symbol of Christ and His church?

2. At some point every Christian is called to submit. To whom are you to submit as a Christian? How does this make you feel? What things can we do to improve our attitude of submission?

3. What is the husband's responsibility in spiritually nurturing his wife? What is the wife's responsibility in helping her husband grow spiritually? Give some specific examples.

4. What three things can you do this week to demonstrate to your partner that you desire to be responsible in your role?

5. What are the commonly conceived roles of men and women in society today? How does the church's understanding of these differ? What effect has society had on the way the church looks at these roles? What effect has the church had on society's view of role distinctions?

6. What is a helpmate? In what areas is the wife called to be a helpmate to her husband? How is she to fulfill this role? What characteristics are seen in a good helpmate?

7. Respond to the following statement:

   The passages in the Bible which refer to the roles of men and women must be seen in their cultural setting. These are not eternal principles, but are culturally bound in the time period in which they were written. To take this message and force it upon today's church is like enforcing head coverings (1 Cor. 11), footwashings (John 13:14-15), or kissing as a Christian greeting (Rom. 16:16). These were just social customs of that day. We may infer principles from these passages but we should not make them authoritative.

8. What emotions are conveyed by the following terms?
    a. Equal Rights Amendment
    b. Feminism
    c. Male chauvinism
    d. Biblical or evangelical feminism
    e. Family role reversal (the husband stays home while the wife pursues a career)

    Why do these terms convey these emotions?